D1027253

Light is sown for the righteous,
and gladness for the upright in heart.

Psalms 97:11

Sown in Light

Sown in Light:
poetry for the forgotten soul

BY TEKIRA BRISCOE

Sown in Light
© 2023 Tekira Briscoe
ISBN: 979-8-9853373-6-5

Published by Mama's Kitchen Press
Austin, TX / Los Angeles, CA
mamaskitchenpress.com

First Trade Paperback Original Edition, 2023

Manufactured in the United States of America

Cover Art by Andile Bokweni
Cover Design by Krystle May Statler
Layout Design by Emily Anne Evans

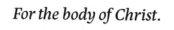

For the body of Christ.

TABLE OF CONTENTS

PART TWO: PULLING WEEDS

PART THREE: PRODUCING PETALS

FOREWORD

This is the book I needed when I was in college, seeking God and figuring out my identity. This book sings the song of those who hang in the balance of living a life that pleases their creator, parents, community, and obligations while trying to simply live their own life. Is it possible to be a multi-faceted human and live a righteous life? Tekira doesn't stray away from the questions that many believers ask and are afraid to ask. This faith lifestyle often comes with more questions than answers, but society assumes that we should know it all. Just because we believe in an all-knowing God does not mean we know it all. There are often times when we question that as well.

Just after college, I used to attend a very strict church. During that time, I devoted nearly every day to the church and its daycare. While I thought it was noble, it wasn't until I left the church and returned home that all questions came. *Why would God allow me to go through that? Is the God who worked miracles thousands of years ago the same God now? Who am I at my core?* Knowing that there is someone else in the world who knows what it is like to question their faith, God, and themselves helps me not to feel alone. If I have found that commonality in Tekira, I know there are others in the world who have felt the same way.

What moved me most in this book is that despite all of the questions, there is a resolve in the end. No matter what your story is, there is a calling from God to *"Try me. Not because you grew up in church, and not because you were told to, but because you want to know me for you. Just try me for a little while, and see how I come through."*

That is the call. Try God. For yourself. See how God comes through for you.

> — *Camari Carter Hawkins, author of* Death by Comb *and founder of Mama's Kitchen Press*

PREFACE

The hardest part of writing this book was believing that it
deserved to be written. Believing these poems would matter
outside the confines of my journey and that someone would
connect with the message is an idea far outside my comfort
zone. How could my words be valuable to others?

The scariest part of writing this book was fearing that I
didn't complete my God-given mission to share words of
encouragement and light, even in the darkest of times. I
feared I didn't fully express my story in a way that doesn't
diminish church culture, my family, or my God, but details
the intimacy and connection between all three.

As you read these poems, you may understand what I mean or
even begin to question my meaning. If you think at any time,
Where is this going, or *Does she still respect God?*, I don't blame
you. My family may even begin to wonder if I have deviated
from the values of the Pentecostal Holiness I have been
brought up on. And I would say those are all fair questions
and thoughts. I, even in my own faith walk, have pondered
the same thing.

I want to assure you that I am still as strong in my faith as I
ever was. I love Jesus so much that when I just think of His
goodness, well, you know the rest. But in this book, I had to
be honest. I had to peel back the layers of the most important
and personal relationship I have, the one between myself

and Jesus. It would have been a disservice to my walk and relationship with God if I wasn't fully transparent about the highs and the lows. It would have been tragic to pretty-up or falsify my testimony in any way. It all deserves to be told.

So yes, I love Jesus, and I still have questions. Yes, I adore the Lord, and I've been angry with Him, too. I still value the traditions I've been taught, and I've also had to let some of them go.

I am wholly on my faith journey, and there is nothing wrong with that. There is power in taking a step back from all the voices around you and listening to the Holy Spirit, reading the Bible for yourself, and asking what's true.

And that's what I did.

This book is for people like me—my people. People of faith. People who have struggled with their faith. People who aren't afraid to feel. People who accept and appreciate honesty. People who have felt isolated and alone, even in the church. People who know that there is a God, but wonder if God knows you. My introverts. My good girls. My church boys. My rebels. My holy rollers. My friends. I see you.

Tekira

Sown in Light

Namesake

I wonder if, when my mother picked the name
for her brown-eyed, chubby-cheeked baby girl,
she knew it meant light bouncing off glitter.

I wonder if she knew
how I would shine
like fireflies kiss my skin.
The moment I touch air,
I spark burning embers of red,
flickering as far as the eye can see.
It's as if I lay on the horizon
between the sky and the sea
then quickly fade
as not to cause the moon to envy
my warmth.

I wonder if my mother knew
I would try to hide my light
by digging trenches
deep enough to bury talents.
Wishing nothing grows
faster than I have bushels to cover it.
I keep it safe under the guise
of humbleness,
hoping it doesn't multiply, so
no one has the chance to uncover it
and discover my treasures.

I wonder if she knew
the responsibility of light would
seem too heavy for my
brown shoulders.
She labeled me
the reflection of my purpose,
called out my energy by name
and placed it in the hands of others
so that they may proclaim my
worthiness of life.

Perhaps she knew exactly who
she would give birth to,
so she named me the one thing
I would try to run from.
They call me
Kira.
I can remember I am already
everything I was afraid to be.

PART ONE:
Planting Seeds

Sunday Morning

I wake up to the sharp, shaky notes
of an off-key soprano in full worship mode.
I hear her matching Donnie beat for a beat,
struggling for the high note.
This could only mean one thing—
it's Sunday morning.

I feel the sunbeams through
the too-thin curtains on my window.
I smell eggs scrambling
and bacon sizzling on the stove.
I reach up in a panic to check that
my silk scarf is still on my head
and listen to the gospel music channel,
switch from Donnie to Vicki.

I roll my body and my eyes at the same time.
I look to my left and
spot the full spread of a Sunday's uniform.
Time to brush and wash every surface of skin,
primp and iron every part of
what will end up being a six-piece outfit
if you count the undergarments.

I slip into my patent-leather shoes with fresh scuffs
on the toes from praise dance rehearsal.
Untie the scarf just right as not to mess up the press
my Granny did last night.

Inhale the scent of grease and burnt hair
touching my shoulders.
I try to flip it over my shoulder as the other girls do
but it's bone straight and as stiff as one too
...I still feel cute.

I have plenty of time to fight with my brother,
switch my cherry lip gloss and hair scrunchies
from my black purse to my heart-shaped one
with the pearl handle,
find stockings that don't have a hole in them, and...

RUN!

Unplug the iron.
Turn off the TV.
Find my Bible.
Accost the front seat.
Pray for safe travels
and nothing but green lights
because
we're 15 minutes late
from being an hour early to church.

Small Churches

Ain't nothing like the small churches
with the wooden, threadbare pews
that seat the faithful families of few.

Churches so small you hear
every high pitch, off-key note
sung in earnest expression.
Hands are lifted up in praise and
looking for a blessin'
clapping off beat to one little drummer boy
who's had no lessons.

Churches so small
the choir consists of the kids
of visiting families and friends,
and when just one person leaves,
we have a praise team again.
The teacher is the preacher,
and the baker is the singer.
The soundman is the deacon,
and everybody takes turns cleanin'
on the weekend.

Churches so small the children
are seen as soldiers on the field.
Holding point and kneeling at altars,
given swordlike scriptures to wield

as they stand alongside older saints
and hide behind their faithful shields.

Churches so small we notice each other,
and we can't hide behind one another.
Every voice is needed, everybody is valued.
And when the faithful few show up to worship,
there's no telling what God will do.

Princesses Aren't Real

I don't recall the exact date my life changed,
but I remember the day.
I know the California sun was shining bright.
I know I walked into the house and tried to
catch my reflection in the freshly waxed dark wood floors.
I know I felt pretty that day.
I know there was a blue couch and
the smell of Skin so Soft wafting in the air.
I know this because it was my favorite place to be.
There, at that house... I was a princess.

One day, my father, the king, sat me down
in all his handsome youth and glory and said,
 "Princess, I have something to tell you.
I have another daughter."

I don't recall all the words I said back,
I just know there was a pause,
a tear inside my chest
and the sound of shattering glass
as my heart hit the bottom of my stomach.
Tears flow down my seven-year-old face.
I was never prepared for such heartbreak.
"I thought I was your only princess,"
are the only words I remember saying.

When out of the back
of the house that once resembled a kingdom,

comes the sister I never knew I wanted.
But at the moment, I wasn't sure how to take her.
Same dark skin.
Same black hair.
Same height.
Same face.
Same age.
I just remember I smiled and said hi to her
as I said goodbye to my self-worth.

The king had just split my crown in two,
I no longer knew who I was.
How could I feel special
when I had just been duplicated?
What's the point of confidence
when I know I can easily be replaced?

On that sunny, California day
in my grandma's living room,
I learned princesses aren't real.

At the Prayer Meeting

I place my hands just right
on top of my chest, closest to where
I'm told the spirit lives.

I bow my head,
tilt it slightly to the left and
peak out the corner of my eyes.

I see arms raise
hands that perfectly bend into cups
as if lifting sacrifices up.

I hear tongues twisting
into unknown words building
a tower of babel to the heavens.

I feel the stillness of the air
prickle the hairs on the back of my neck
with awareness
that at any moment...

A cry could be released
from agony or rapture
and tears could no longer be held, hostage
but free to dance on the face of their oppressor.

The biggest ego in the room could tremble,
the strongest knees at the pew could buckle,

either from the lifting of their burdens
or the from the weight of their struggles.

The tightest lips might wave with praise,
the deepest secrets may come out to bathe
in the cleansing...

At any moment, facades could fade
and we'll be left barely standing on our own
transparent and alone next to each other

no makeup
no shoes
no hat
no suit

just hands
and kees
and heads
and mouths

observing the quiet of the temple
before the spirit breaks out,

I place my feet just right
at the bench closest to the altar,
and with bated breath,
I wait for the praying to start.

Just Might Let You Grow

I am as dark as black sapphire but appear as vibrant as yellow.

I am as soft as dandelions but feel strong as a grain of sand caught between the fingertips brave enough to hold me.

Still, I would rather be loose and unbound flowing wherever the wind blows.
I love tender touches and honey drips down my curves. Oils that make me shine and glisten from a distance. I am not opposed to the burning coal and velvet soul of tradition, but I crave independence.

I dream of love that looks like full acceptance. I dream of having the confidence to be me in season and out, even when I'm popular or when I'm questioned.

I am as crafty as homemade flower arrangements and as common as the green grass they are plucked from.

But I often worry I am not enough.

I wish others saw the beauty that is me, uninhibited. When they look at me, I want them to see a life full of bounce and sprite. I want to be a symbol of freedom and creativity, like nature's own frenzied masterpiece made with passion, unique and wild.

I often lay awake at night, wondering if I change, would people still revere me as the same vision as before? Or is my attraction only because I coincide with the expectations of my ancestors?

The best thing I could ever do is grow into treating myself as a temple. Only allow nourishment to enter my gates, erect walls of confidence to withstand the harsh winds of criticism and learn to dwell in the tenderness of my solitude.

I feel guilty for wanting to change. I have built a presence of positivity and local fame yet I want to start fresh. Is it wrong to recreate my image in a new era of self-discovery? Does going against tradition mean I'm not as appealing as I "should" be?

I often worry I am not enough.

The Sound Puberty Makes

I remember black hair wrapped over hair
and falling to my chin.
I remember black-rimmed glasses and frames so thin
perched on my nose.
I remember my first pair of high heels
bringing me two inches closer to womanhood.
I remember the soft smiles and whispers of acknowledgment
from those on the other side of adolescence.
I remember feeling as if I were crossing some rite of passage
from a child into young adulthood.
I remember feeling proud.

click clack, click, clack

I remember wearing my heels to church.
I remember cold white tiles
and the smell of cookies in the dining hall.
I remember Sis Dean, teaching me in her gentle voice
and beautiful smile that a lady knows how to walk in heels.
I remember walking the line where the tiles meet,
one foot in front of the other, shoulders back, head high.
I remember the sound my heels made
echoing off the cold, empty room.

click clack, click, clack

I remember going home and walking

the edges of the sidewalk, the beam of the sandbox,
the painted lines in the parking lot.

click clack, click, clack

I remember, my friends would say,
"She walks like she's grown."
I remember putting the heels aside,
changing into flats and slides, sweatpants, hair tied.
I remember being complimented on the way I walk.
I remember the young girl, walking white tile lines
in the kitchen in the back of the church.
I smile and sway.

click clack, click, clack

Meet Me in a Dance

It starts as a flicker of a movement
in the center of your chest.
Begins to crawl up, looking for a way out,
it aims for your extremities.
Your blood begins to rush,
troubling the waters of baptismal in your gut.
Your hand raises from your side,
grasping the manna falling from the sky.
You bolt from your seat
because the pew cannot contain the glory.
Your cup runneth over as you enter the gates of Holy.
The praise is getting higher,
your feet are getting lighter
to the beat of chains falling.
Heaven comes down,
and you feel power over you,
causing a dip in your left side
and arms to extend right.
You try to find your balance,
but your knees wobble in excitement.
Your body convulses in awkward angles
looking for the best way to untangle
the mess of emotions you feel.
Your heart picks up the pace.
The adrenaline continues to build
and before you can get to an open space,

you dance
jump
twist
turn
spin
run
fall
hum
bend
shout
scream out—
Hallelujah!

Daydreaming

In my young mind,
God is a distant memory
from a lifetime before life,
a mythological creature more truth than myth.
I always picture His hair soft and coiling,
motivating the galaxies to bend.
His feet wide and strong
as gravity demands our subjection,
with hands big enough to craft the sun,
dot craters in the sky,
sprinkle stars like dust.
And His voice is as soft as a single stream
tip-toeing off a mountain's edge.

In my little heart,
He's bright like a kaleidoscope of colors,
colors I never even knew existed.
He sounds like a word
before the world had a name
and there was no language to express grace,
no feelings to contain love,
no mercy to extend.
He's shaped like the forever
that infinity wishes to be—
which is,
which was,
which is to come...

I am fascinated by His existence,
concerned with His omnipotence,
hesitant about His omniscient—
in awe of the God in my mind.
I wonder if He's that incredible in real life.

More Precious

I used to regard her
as nothing more than a mystery,
an entity I was told about
a secret I had to promise to keep
was a path into my soul, no doubt
the most beautiful thing I would ever own.

As she develops, I begin
to better understand her presence.
Her power.
Why people likened her to a flower,
precious, pretty, and promising.
Drawing the boys like bees hoping
to assist her to full bloom.
I learned I had to protect her
from those who assume
she needs their help at all.

I guard her scarcity with a fierceness
for as long as I want to.
I'll place a value on her too high for anyone to pay.
And if I meet the man I feel deserving of her,
I've decided I still won't give her away.
I will share her, between my soul and his,
letting her be the bridge
to oneness and the love, we chose to give.

Conversations in the Shower

How many showers will it take
to wash the shadow of
foreign objects from my body?

How long will I have to sit under
the water, tracing the trail of
invisible fingers along my waist?

My vagina has never felt so
disgustingly immaculate or alone
and unsafe.

Hmm—maybe it depends on how long
a touch can linger after it's
supposed to have gone away.

While there is no evidence of a violation
and no proof that they ever existed,
the hairs on the back of my neck still feel it.

Well, maybe I'm exaggerating,
and the idea of what could have been
is more burning than what was just

a touch,
a grasp,
a handful, if you will.

I tell myself
I'm fine.
I'm here.
It wasn't that bad.
Others have had it worse.
How loud do I have to say it,
before I can convince my body to relax
and my nerves to stop shaking?

I have never felt so aware
of a piece of unbroken skin.

To Keep the Spirits Away

My bedtime routine consists of

Reading one chapter in the Bible
preferably from Psalms or Proverbs,
then placing it under my pillow.

Listening to two gospel songs of worship
with my headphones and CD player,
turning the volume low.

Praying three times, earnestly pleading,
hoping if I say it hard enough,
the nightmares will leave me alone.

Then lying in the dark,
trying to convince my body
to slow the beating of my heart.

Trying to convince my mind that
the sweat on my forehead is
only from doing too much before bed.

Trying to convince my faith
that it is bigger than my fear.
God heard me, and he's already near.

Trying to convince myself that this night,
out of all the nights before,
is the first time I won't have this fight.

Trying to stay awake, only to sleep
and wake up disappointed
that God couldn't even save me in my dreams.

My Superpower is...

every unrung phone on the weekends
every uninvited girl's night out
every single unasked request to dance,
has been etched on the outer layer of my bones
enabling me to move through life
with the assuredness that I am invisible

a very close cousin to the definition of dispensable
I am neither fiery passion nor cool detachment
but I fall somewhere in the middle
like coffee that is neither hot nor iced,
I've gone unnoticed throughout my life

I'm so invisible that ninjas wish
they could unmove earth like me
I can go so unseen that when I cry
my tears are counted as condensation from the sky
I'm so spiritually covert that I am the envy
of all rule-breaking teens
my heart could break in a room full of people
and no one would notice me bleed

every best friend who never called first
every time I was left out of the group chat
every person that likes me on paper
has seeped into the folds of my brain
whispering anti-love notes that I don't matter

Mama Prayed

When the devil went to the throne,
my mother's spirit was already there,
rebuking every evil suggestion,
casting down every demonic intention,
holding onto every Bible-given promise,
going toe-to-toe,
matching scripture for scripture
with the oh-so-subtle spirit of indifference.
If God decided to remove the hedge,
I still had a wall of mama's prayers to protect me,
her hands to lift me,
her voice to strengthen me.

Don't stop praying, Mama,
I need it.

Torn

I don't know if anyone has ever felt like me,
caught between tradition and the Spirit
confusing culture for religion
and feeling misrepresented
in every way.

Too saved to fit in
because the way my conviction is set up
has made me stand out.

Too young to sit with the seasoned saints
because although I praise,
I don't fully understand their shout.

I feel as if I'm just here,
floating between realities.

Loving God too much to rebel,

but heartbroken because
the loneliness is still real.

I can't ignore one or the other
two sides of me warring against each other.

I'm not too impressed by the world,
but the church makes me feel... smothered?

I know I do in my heart
I just don't know,
if I love the Christian piece.
But when it's all I know,
I definitely know how to act the part.

PART TWO:
Pulling Weeds

If I lose my faith,
that's smaller than a mustard seed
how will I ever find it again?
I'm beginning to think,
I never really had it to begin with.

Crisis of Faith

I remember the day I dropped my faith in the middle of the women's section of a Kohl's department store. I swear I felt my pressure drop as it fell out of my chest and rolled on the ground. I could feel the color drain from my face while I stood in the center of the aisle between the Apt 9 dresses and Daisy Fuentes jeans. I felt naked. I had go-backs on one hand, life crisis on the other. What the hell had just happened?

It felt like my body had been slammed against the very foundation I had walked on for all these years, leaving me breathless. Sweat beaded on my forehead and transformed into tears that rolled down my cheeks. (To this day, I think they were running away from a newly wretched and faithless soul like me.)

I remember I started to panic and my hands began to shake. Hangers clattered against each other, reverberating through the air as if they were alerting the heavens. "A life is at stake!" And it was. This ghost of a revelation halted my life. I paused to decide my next move.

By the time the garments fell from my fingers and floated to the ground, I was telling my manager I had to go. There was a life and death emergency, and I needed to leave. With the recent realizations tumbling around the hollowness of my mind, I ran outside, stumbling between life as I knew it and an alternate reality — another reality that I never really considered before, but felt so real to me at the moment:

I didn't have to be saved.
I didn't have to follow Jesus.
I didn't have to go to church every Sunday.
And now that I'm an adult,
did I even really want to?

The way I grabbed my purse and jacket is the way I wish I could have just picked up my faith and left with the security of knowing it would be everything I needed to get to the next destination in life. Instead, I walked robotically to my car, knees trembling.

I put my head on the steering wheel and sobbed. Tears and snot raced down my face to my chin, dripping in my lap—my care runneth over. Anyone passing by would have thought I lost my mind, but I would have had to correct them. I wasn't losing my mind. I was losing my faith. My foundation. My traditions. My culture. My beliefs.

In the middle of my evening shift at a Kohl's department store, my heart cracked as I once again turned down an invitation to go out with coworkers after work. I was a church girl. I didn't drink or go to hookah lounges or hang out with people who did those things. And those weren't the only things I felt I had to say no to.

In my young life, I had learned to turn down everything from dates to parties to social gatherings. Anything that may have

even slightly suggested I didn't have the utmost respect for
God. When I rejected the third invitation to have a social life, I
felt it deep in my mind:

I can't do this anymore.

I was tired. I was tired of it all.
I didn't want to miss things
because I always had to go to church on Sunday.
I was tired of feeling outcast and alone.
I was tired of slinking through religious minefields
so as not to offend people,
tempering my mood when some folks
really should have been cussed out.
I didn't want to deny my flesh
when I didn't exactly know what that meant.
I've been about God since I was six,
before my flesh had time to fully develop
and reveal itself for me to know I would even want to deny it.
I didn't know how long I could keep up
this standard of tradition.
I felt suffocated by the weight
of familial and church expectations.
I didn't get the freedom people so freely speak of.
Freedom from what?
Because all I felt was lonely, suffocated, and let down.

And with those thoughts hanging on the fringes of my brain, I
cried. And prayed. Still holding on to the belief that there is a
God, but with doubt that I wanted to follow him.

Dear God,

I am ready to walk away.
I hate my life.
I don't like who I am or where I'm at.
I'm so unhappy.
I know you're real.
I know you're true.
But I feel suffocated and
I'm starting to resent you.
Oh, Jesus,
what am I going to do?

I sat there, in the darkening parking lot of a vast shopping center, and allowed my heart to bleed from the hole faith had left in my chest.

For the first time since I could remember,
I knew I had a choice.

Who Am I?

Absent of water,
out from under the umbrella of convention,
drying in the waves of indecision,
outside the margins of my mother's saved home,
walking in the daytime alone?

Who am I, minus the purple pews
and stained glass windows,
without the seven a.m. Sunday wake-up time,
after the obligatory six a.m. prayer lines?

Who am I, when I don't have to be anyone,
when the seeds planted begin to take root
and tangle with the truth
that my life is my own?

I gasp for air.
but I don't know if I am dying or just learning to breathe.
How well did I inhale before this moment?

Sympathy

If God remains the same,
why is my life ever-changing?
The God in joy, the God in pain,
the God in sorrow.
This God proclaims to be
steadfast, immovable.,
the same yesterday and today.

But yesterday, I felt sunshine,
saw butterflies dancing in the wind,
felt Earth's breath against my skin.
And today, it's pouring rain, so long
and so hard.
My Bible is dripping with tears

that make puddles on the floor,
that turn into streams and
 flow into Galilee,
a sea I can't walk on.

I can see through the atheists' eyes the disparity
between the good and the truly evil.
With all this disease in the world,
where is God when you need him?
Did you come to save the sick and shut-in?
The hopeless and helpless, homeless and hungry?
Rape and slavery and pain and sadness?

Is a God who allows this
one that I can even stand with?

I expect you to answer when I call!
I made sacrifices and all.
Prayed and praised and
bowed and raised hands.
I did what I was supposed to do.
But everything is changing so fast,
I have whiplash.
It may seem crass, but I just need to ask, which God are you?

The same, the same but nothing on Earth fits that.
You said to be consistent, but your creation goes against that.
You're the ruler right?
The alpha and the omega?
The same God of Abraham, Isaac, and Jacob.
The same one who poured a plague on creation?
If you're the same God who in Genesis saw
that it was good, then why is the sanctity
of nature and oneness of humanity so misunderstood?

I'm not an atheist, I can never be.
I just understand their hesitancy
a little more deeply than before.

Places I Have Lived

I have lived in the breath
of the good Lord's whispers
Brought to the water's edge
led there by my mother's prayer
I made a home between dimensions

I have lived in the belly of the fish
cradled through galvanic currents
floating on tides of selfish desires
I made a bed of self-righteousness

I have lived on the outskirts of my skin
exiled by delusive intentions
overflowing with suppressed ambitions
I made a sanctuary of isolation

I have lived in the recesses of forsaken wisdom
I have lived on the ridges of broken humanity
I have lived beneath the tinges of purpose

I have lived
I have Lived
I have LIVED .... in places,
only God would dare to go

If I Go

If I go into this space any further , I might not come back.
I may find the bottom of that rock
or catch a glimpse of the underbelly of the beast.
I may just make my bed next to him
out of sticks of criticism and leaves of doubt.
Add some cushy denial and let life work itself out,
absent of my participation.

If I go longer without sunlight,
I may just find when I look at the darkness long enough,
it also illuminates,
shining black and bleak on my faith.
I may find the dark is cold and loving,
keeping me awake enough so I never dream all the way.
REM sleep is only for people of faith.

If I go further into my loneliness
and wrap my arms around myself,
esteem may just leave me
Tired of this threesome with misery,
she will let me wallow in the darkness.

If I go further into depression,
I may just get comfortable and stay.

This burden weighs on my fingertips,
denying my hands their partnership.
I don't recall the last time
They joined together in prayer.

Doubt is heavy.

Cursed

Have you ever tasted something
so bitter and disgusting
It makes you stick your tongue out
and squinch your nose?
Gag a little and twist your face
because the assault on your sense was,
so unexpected
so unwelcomed
that you regret the 10 seconds
it takes for the flavor leave your mouth?
That's what fuck tasted like to me.
Like stale kale with no sauce.
Shit smelled like shit.
Once I said it the sound assaulted my nose.
I tried bitch and damn too.
It came off like a child trying to eat new foods,
smacking and licking and choking on the flavors,
the words too heavy and sour to savor.

So I tried nibbling on the edges of profanity,
starting with small words like hell.
Nope.
Let me hide them in my sentences...
Maybe if I sprinkle it over a phrase...
Say it timid and shy.
Yell it loud and bold.
Try it with emotion.
Season it with power.
FUCK
BULLSHIT
DAMN
Yeah,
it still sucks.
I sound broken.
I look dumb.
sigh
Even when I try to be "unsaved"
I can't even cuss right
Forget it

Lip Service

This is the part of the story where I say all the obligatory
phrases reserved for #churchlife.

If they say: God is good
I say: All the time
They say: And all the time
I say: God is good

They ask: How are you doing?
I say: I'm blessed and highly favored.

Instead of: I don't know.

My confidence is unraveling like the thread hanging from
the back of the pew, still curled in submission as the threader
intended. It's unnoticeable until it extends, hoping some
curious hand will pull or push it back in place again. That's
me, extendedly numb, waiting for the force whichever way it
comes to determine my place.

They ask: How's life treating you?
I say: I can't complain.

Instead of: I feel beat up.

I'm full of the adrenaline rush of fighting with myself, for myself. It's not easy to overcome a mind with every belief to lose or that overtakes a thought constantly on the move. I am tired, weak, distressed, depressed, but I smile, joke, suggest, and finesse my punches into measures of dance. I sit still and look pretty instead of showing the mess that I am.

My lips are unfamiliar with naked truths.
Those muscles have never been used
for anything other than compliances
and other pleasantly molded words:
Yes, ma'am.
No, ma'am.
Praise the Lord.
Hallelujah.
Amen.
Yes, I can.
I will be there.
You can have it.
Put my name on the list.
I can help.
See how easily the words form
without help from my heart?

These lips are so good
at servicing everyone else
except me.

I don't have night terrors anymore;
I barely sleep.

How I Envy Eve

Before her descent into modesty
Post creation
Pre-slip
Sans bra
Oblivious to salvation
The time in eternity where nudity had no sexualization,

I imagine her breasts swung whichever way the wind blew,
nipples accustomed to the warmth of the sun
I think her spine curved
when tickled by the leaves falling off the tree

I believe her body danced in sync
with the ebb and flow of the sea
She and man and beast were the same
Baring teeth
Showing skin
Laying free
Running blind
Living full

She was who I was meant to be

We Weren't Friends

but when he smiled
I became curious
on the other end
of such a grin.
He moved like freedom
and beckoned like a sin.
My spirit was bothered,
unlike my countenance.
Temptation was calling
but it came from within.

We weren't serious,
But when he called,
I came more than once.
My eyes followed his
tiptoeing fingertips
shaded from the sun.
He traced blooming
flower petals
making rivers run.
He watered sprouting
green fields
causing bees to come.
Honey flowed from
every direction by
the time he was done.

And like sunshine after rain
my body sighed in relief
then my spirit burned in pain.
All the same, I laid there
resisting repentance.
As I came, I stayed there
testing independence.
When I left I said a prayer
not for forgiveness.
But I asked the Lord if
he could remove,
the burden of conviction.

How Long Will I

How many times will I look for G-o-d
in between the letters of "what's his name"?
Or search in the cracks of his colorful language
to pick up the pieces of my worth?
How long will I hold his hand,
hoping to complete a self-portrait
I can stand hanging on my walls?
How many times will I stretch my standards
until they emulate suggestions?
Or contort my peace
to match the pieces of his emotional fragility?
I guess the real question is…
how long will I use his sins,
to hide from me?

Dear God

When I look at your reflection,
I am often confused
about your presence in my life.
Would you rather I call you God or Father?

As God, you are the father, and
a father is an embodiment of your love,
often regarded as a reflection
of your paternal affection toward us.
Yet fatherless children don't
experience you as a father.
You're more of a faceless
entity from above.

For some of us,
you resemble
a judge,
or a bum,
or a thug,
or a deadbeat.
Should I call you God,
the Good Father,
or the Man Who Left Me?

The pathway to trust you has been paved with
broken promises glittering like good intentions.

I see the suggestion of parenting but
feel the impression of forced independence.
I feel hello hugs and kisses
to mend disappearing acts and random goodbyes.
I see the shadow of the entity that you are.
I know the truth of your lies.
I know you more in theory than actual function.
You're more fable than nonfiction,
more the lesson than the teacher.

When I look in your mirror,
I see a man half-created
with a gaping heart,
leaky eyes,
wide smile,
and velvet words.
I don't trust your reflection.
So how can I take you at your word?

If a father is a reflection of your image,
then God, your image may need work.

Sincerely,
Broken Daughter

If all you had to do to heal was forgive, would you?

Don't make it sound so easy...

As if it's not like breaking the bones of a celestial body and moving it from one universe to another to rediscover how to balance on a new axis.

As if it's not like calling into question my very existence, which, by definition, is the continuation of a life I built on a foundation of protecting my significance.

If all I had to do was give up ALL I HAD and lose everything I used to conserve myself and preserve my mental health...

Then I am left gaping, open and sensitive to introspection, digging deep into the wound to ascertain the infection of my spirit.

Don't act like healing isn't one of the hardest things
I will ever have to do.

If forgiveness is all that stands in the way,
if forgiveness is the only thing my soul still lacks,
if forgiveness is the answer to my future surpassing my past,
then I must drop the face of the mask I've had to date.
This is more than just letting go.

I have to fully amputate pieces of my consciousness to rebuild
my subconscious thoughts and create a new cognition.

I have to ignore my flighty intuition that often confuses
butterflies with the beautiful lie that I deserve to be given
some kind of consolation prize for my pain in the name of an
apology.
If I forgive,
then that would be the death of me.
I'd have to answer for who I chose to be,
stand skeletal in front of the mirror and acknowledge the
pain of my soul laboring for rebirth.

Breathe in and out,
    feel the sweat fall down my brow,
        bare my teeth and push until it all falls out,
            the bitterness, resentment, anger, fear.

    Don't make it sound like healing isn't the hardest thing
        I will ever have to do.

If all I had to do was give up everything I thought I knew about
faith and strength and choose to start anew, would I do it?

Pretty Please

I asked you to let me go.
Let me leave it all behind,
the cares,
the f****,
pack up my wander and lust
and skip over the valley
of indecision.
Dance in the cooling winds
of inhibition.
Party with the stars
at night.
Embrace the intensity
of spotlight.
Hair gone,
legs out
Breasts swinging,
smile wide,
confidence on-fleek.
Unearthing the person that
is the real me.
So why are you stopping me?
I asked you to let me go.

Who are you?
Jesus with all these questions,
I'm starting to think
I never really knew you at all.

Prove to Me

God, I need you to do something,
because I am ready to let it all go.
My hands are so slippery with tears.
I feel your promises running through them.
My feet are so tired from standing still,
my toes are numb, waiting for my miracle.

DO SOMETHING.
Crack the sky with a bolt of lightning
and let the oceans that rise in praise,
wave hello to my drying belly.
Where water and fire once converged
to a spiritual spring shape,
we now have the searing lands of weary pleas.
I am tired of asking.
But please,

MOVE SOMETHING.
As if the very stone on my chest
is the same one that stood
in the way of your tomb
and kept my spirit hell-bound.
My womb is open for your presence
to fill it,
but I am feeling barren, as if you sealed it,
shut from ever bearing the fruit requested of me.
I hope this is not too much, but...

BREAK SOMETHING.
If you must.
I offer myself as tribute.
Consider me the law that must be broken
so that others may be healed.
Make me as the prophecies fulfilled,
whole and completely intertwined in your will.

I just need to know, even in now,
you still see me.

PART THREE:
Producing Petals

Blue Sunday

I woke up that Sunday morning to the light shining through the sheer brown curtains of my bedroom window. The sound of 90s gospel music playing on the TV in the next room over tickled my consciousness. I recognized the sound of water running and footsteps moving up and down the hallway in quick succession for morning showers. The air was filled with getting-ready-for-church-activity... hustle, bustle, prayer, and the occasional "Have you seen my..." question from my uncle or cousin. This routine had been the same since I could remember and normally, I was right in the thick of it, moving, singing, and dressing. But that Sunday, I sat on the edge of the bed, laid my head in my hands, and made a decision... *This is the last time I go to church.*

I paused for the minute it took that resolution to circulate throughout my body. I closed my eyes and hoped the resolve settled and filled the cracks of my broken heart, steeling me against the feelings of fear and guilt that tried to bubble up. I slid my feet into my old pink slippers and slowly made my way across the hall to the now steam-filled bathroom, all the while saying... *This is the last time I go to church.* Convincing myself that this was the best thing I could do for myself.

What more time did I have to waste on actionless faith? God had been good to me but I had nothing left to give him other than my goodbyes. Selfish as that seemed it felt like the most honorable thing I could do, leave before I was charged with hypocrisy. Exit before I added to the further embarrassment of Christianity. Bow out before I was bowed over in shame and discomfort of a tainted character... And besides, I wasn't as committed as some of the other saints. I had too many questions, and too many unfulfilled prayers and I wasn't sure what else there was for me to do, but leave.

So on that Sunday, I decided I would go to church, sit on the left side, in the second pew, towards the center aisle like I always did and say...what? Goodbye? I wasn't sure of the exact words I would use.

I just knew that time would be a silent, defining moment for him and me. No one else would know that we were breaking up. There would be no announcement, just a sweep of his name from my everyday vocabulary. People would just look up and notice I didn't talk about him as much. I would stop mentioning his name. I wouldn't go to the church family functions anymore and my habits would change. I didn't know what they would be changed too because it was abundantly apparent to me that I didn't fit in with the world either... but the point was that I would be different. Better? I don't know. But different nonetheless.

By the time I made the hour-long drive to S Figueroa St and pulled up to the white church trimmed in brown, with purple pews and stained glass windows, I was shaky. My hands were sweating and the tears were already flowing. I sat quietly the whole service, praying. Grieving. Pouring. It was the quietest, most lonely, understated funeral service I had ever been to.

The euology, I mean benediction, happened rather quickly.
And as soon as we were free to go, I dipped. Out the side door,
towards the left side parking lot, towards my periwinkle car
with the missing rims, and pulled off.

No fellowship.
No atmosphere.
No basking in his presence.
No soft gospel music.
No feelings of fulfillment and peace.

Just me and space and time. Dang.

Lamenting the Cloudy Sky

How did I come away from that season of
loss,
depression,
and hurt?

How am I still here clinging to the cross,
kneeling in His cleansing blood,
staring grace face to face, and
opening my arms wide to embrace the life of a believer?

I was driving in my car,
enveloped in silence and lamenting the cloudy sky.
Going in a direction I don't remember.
Running from a life I tried to forget.
Contemplating the abyss of numbness,
I found myself floating when the sun broke the sky
and light began to fill the space around me.

I turned my face to feel the rays warm my cheeks.
I gave a deep sigh and a still, small voice spoke to me:

Try me.
Not because you grew up in church,
and not because you were told to,
but because you want to know me for you.
Just try me for a little while, and see how I come through.

It All Started with a Lie

I researched anger today,
after I took a sip of the
poison handed to me.
Felt my insides incinerate like
the fire to rubber and weed,
not realizing rage was just
a mark of shame.

I researched shame
after I hid in the recesses of my mind,
blocked the light and let cynicism grow
like mold over time, until
the stench became too much to bear,
not realizing the discomfort in my own skin
was a symptom of insecurity.

I researched insecurity
the dormant emotion that pulled my spirit
down into the ocean's depths,
covered me in waves of fear and agitation
until my cells were panting for air.

Not realizing the self-doubt
was a symptom of deception.

Deceiving myself into believing
I was never enough to begin with.

God Met Me in the Form of Exhaustion

I am tired of dancing around
the fringes of indecision.
I am no longer willing to live my life
balancing on the threads
of good intentions and ignoring conviction.
I am created to live differently.
I am predestined, and although hesitant,
I can't unring the call I received from the womb.
I won't succumb to what He has already overcome.
I am tired of fighting.
No more hiding from the light.

I will do things differently this time.
I will build our relationship for myself
with prayer on prayer, precept on precept.
I will rely on experience more than philosophy,
Bible more than theology.
I will read the word before I search for one.
I will not bend the word to fit inside the curves
of my heart.

I will give you me, like
lovers do in the act of loving.
I will bare my soul and engage with passion,
minus the need to perform.
With no lips to service
and no obligation to fulfill,
I will offer myself as an empty vessel,
trembling from your graces, overflowing
filling the cracks of my unworthiness.
I surrender.

Hope

It is not a bright light
but a distant glow.
It hangs in our peripheral vision,
beckoning such a visceral,
reaction
that begrudgingly, we follow.
Too tired to stop today.
Maybe we'll stop tomorrow.

Oh Israel

the audacity of you to wrestle
God with unclean hands
the gall of your unseasoned lips
to fix themselves in such a way
to take in air
wrap around the vowels
complete full diction to say...
I won't let go... until you bless me
how bold
how brave
how necessary

three-thousand years later and
I can almost taste the sweat on your brow
I can hear the song of a struggle,
the high whistles of pain through your teeth
the low groans of labored breathing from your nose
I imagine you sound like *Total Praise*

In my mind
I can see the contracting of your muscles
I see the dirt under your fingernails
the rips in your clothes as they're pulled to and fro
the blood from your skin trickling and
hoping to be cleansed
you look like a sheep fighting to be a sacrifice
how aged

how graceless
how stained

my heart calls to you
egging you on
pushing you to fight
pulling for your victory
grit your teeth
steel your brow
and hold
this is better than hope
this the faith that exposes God's
mercy and love and grace

rumble old man
rumble
and when you're done
... tag me in

Prayer Is...

P(ersistent)
O(pen)
E(xpectant)
T(hankful)

The folding of your will into His until His will is all there is.

The clasping of your hands onto His word until they nestle in
the cracks of your ego, filling you up so that your peace may
not seep through.

The laying down of all pretense and past tense reassured that
God doesn't work in common sense.

The petitioning of the throne,

    the knocking on the door,

      the calling,

        the asking,

          the seeking until God shows up again,

            once more.

Come Over

Ay,
Come thru.
I just want to spend time with you.

Uhhhh the sound of his words slid down my nerves like
honey
tickling every ending and sparking the beginning of a hot
flash.
Not a second passed before I was transported back in time,
my senses taken on a ride.

My lips could anticipate the wetness of his kiss.
My lips could hardly await the softness of his lips.
My hands could feel his muscles flex and retract.
My fingers could trace the mole on his back.
My nostrils widen at the thought of his cologne.
My body tingles at the sound of his raspy tone

and if I close my eyes
I can even hear an almost imperceptible moan...
or wait...
is that a groan? a growl?
A frustrating rumble in my belly
that can either be hunger or grief
my innards at war with my flesh telling me to
KEEP
IT
TOGETHER!

As I open my eyes, I look around my room for a way of escape.
Instead, I see keys to a car with a full tank of gas,
a bonnet just removed from freshly wrapped hair,
and a wallet with last Friday's paycheck still in it.

Dang.

I take a breath and say the only thing I could think to say,
"Sorry, I can't cum... I mean COME... over anymore."

The Breakup Note

I hope you know I appreciate what you have done.
Thank you for helping me stay alert
and aware of my surroundings.
You've kept me on my toes
in more ways than one
for most of my life.
On some level, I felt safe with you.
You were constant.
Never too far from my mind,
always lingering behind to remind me to never be
too loud,
too bold
too bright,
too smart,
too beautiful,
too happy.
Because your job
as my closest companion,
is to protect me from the scary and unfamiliar.

But in doing that,
you've also kept me from the grand and purposeful.
Hold me back from the exhilarating and successful.
I've never had the privilege to jump off the cliff
and discover that I have eagle's wings.
Or dive head first into shark-infested waters
and let sharks know they should be scared of me.

You didn't let me test my faith so it can be proven faithful
you took the place of my God in my life...

So although we've been close,
I have to let you go.
I have to run away and escape into open waters
swim in the ocean to know that I am capable of surviving

I've started dating love and faith.
I like it.
I like them.
I'm falling in love with them,
and I hate to break it to you like this anxiety,
but I don't need you anymore.
It's not you, it's me.
I'm ready to move on,
and we're too toxic for each other at this stage in my life.
I hope you understand.

Best Wishes,

Me

Relationship Goals

I talk to him
daily,
stretch out my hand
and caress the imprint of his form
with my fingertips.
I connect with him in a way
that leaves me breathless,
leaves me uncomfortable
in the assured way he directs me.
He knows me
Speaks my thoughts before they become words.
Massages my nerves to loosen the grip
anxiety tries to hold me with.
Holds me up, accountable
when temptation begins to smell
like sandalwood and chocolate.
He fills me with his love.
I pray he never leaves.
Even when I doubt him,
he's forever there, patient and kind,
even in his correction.
He tugs on my gut,
whispers sweet everythings in my ear
until he knows I hear him.
He is a manifestation of the best love I've ever known.
He is the greatest gift I've ever received

Re-gifting

Here I have a re-gift for you
Covered in tinsel and ribbons
Hand-wrapped in velvet luxury
Kissed closed and whispered shut
Packaged with just enough bubble wrap
so as to not crack the fragile material
Put some respect on the packaging
Don't rip it open
The contents are sharp
They are explosive and sensitive to the ear
If mishandled, they can cause damage to your organs
Become a weight on your heart
Vice around your lung
A pit in your stomach
A noose around your neck
The damage could be irreversible
Please handle your opinions with care

Dead Ends

I cut my hair to see if God was real.
Shaved the sides because
the taste of freedom made me high.

I watched
as tradition fell to the ground
like tired leaves.
If only they would get swept away.
It would save me the effort
of picking them up
and throwing away all that I know.
Maybe if it evaporated
like puffs of black smoke,
I can say with a clear conscious
tradition left on its own.

I cut my hair so when the sun shone,
the rays would
seep into my brain,
chasing away ill thoughts.
I lined up my edges to
make my ideas
presentable before Him.

I thought
if only I could sense God on my scalp,
remove the barrier between
my mind and grace,
I could lay prostrate on the ground,
feel the footsteps of mercy walk by
then cry out, knowing this time,
I did not miss Him.

I had to cut my hair
so that faith could grow anew.
I snipped the mane
of heavy expectations
to let the mustard seed
feel the rain from the sky.
No longer choked by the
strands of spiraling anxiety.
I knew,
if only I had no more dead ends
I could show my face, lay bare my skin.
Drop vanity for His name's sake,
pick up freedom in its place.

When Did We Become Awkward - Part 1

I saw her late one torrid afternoon
springing through the air-conditioned valley mall
with the same bright smile
that I remember from vacation bible school.
The same brown skin
as when she sat next to me on Sunday mornings
on the 4th row left side behind the first lady
and the deacon wives.
I would recognize that slick-back ponytail and
side-swept bang from anywhere.

She saw me and her cheeks hesitated to reach her eyes.
Her lips mouthed the words hi, as her hand just almost waved.
And before I could return the gesture,
she abruptly turned her back and proceeded down the aisle.
Leaving behind my crest-fallen face and stuttering heart.

I didn't know what to do.
Should I have run after her,
reached out, and grazed the back of her hand?
Should I have raised her chin and called her name?
Or at the very least
displayed my scars so she knew we've all felt shame?
I should have said...

… I love you…still.

Even though I wonder,
would it have even mattered?

When Did We Become Awkward - Part 2

clumsily wielding the titles sinner and "saint"
as if either word could fully encompass
the complexities of our faith

when did we become strangers
bypassing smiles and cheerful greetings
like we both weren't in the same soil
feeling triumphs and fielding beatings

when did we become bitter
our scents sharp and disagreeable
as if the choice each of us made
to the other is inconceivable

when did the silence between us
become a desert of unspoken words
instead of the fertile ground
where our truths could grow undisturbed

When did our honesty turn us into enemies
Poised for the defense of our feelings
Instead of leading us to seek peace and healing
I wonder when...
When?
When?

No One Has Ever Called a Butterfly Ugly

No one has ever denied them their right to grow.
No one has ever halted their season of change.
nor have they criticized their phases of life
and then labeled them a butterfly's trait.

Just because a butterfly was once a caterpillar,
we don't say it's "acting brand new."
Just because a caterpillar moves like no other animal,
we don't ignore its uniqueness.

From the filling of their bellies
to the cocooning of their bodies
in drool-spun silk.
We watch with confident eyes,
wait with cooling breaths
 for the process to be over.
We applaud them for evolving.

4 AM

Dew touches so lightly, it feels like a dream
tugging on my subconscious mind.
Eyes crack open to see the blueish-gray
light filtering through the blinds.
They close for a second chance at sleep.

Cold floors shoot shivers up my spine.
Blankets get thrown over the shoulders.
There's no sound but the sun waking up and
a tender breeze drifting through the air
in the dead of night.
I kneel in obedience,
bow in reverence,
too tired to move my lips,
but my posture acknowledges his presence.

Romans 8: 25-28

*But if we hope for what we do not yet have, we wait for it patiently.
In the same way, the Spirit helps us in our weakness. We do not
know what we ought to pray for, but the Spirit himself intercedes
for us through wordless groans. And he who searches our hearts
knows the mind of the Spirit, because the Spirit intercedes for
God's people in accordance with the will of God. And we know that
in all things God works for the good of those who love him, who
have been called according to his purpose.*

The House

If I can just get to the house.
Weary eyelids open on command,
fluttering like fragile butterfly wings
before my tired spirit could slow their ascent.
My body feels shallow and empty.
My feet remind me of little,
so each step out of the room feels non-existent.

If I can just get to the house.
My body reacts on autopilot.
Thank God my muscles remember,
because I sure have forgotten what
Sunday-morning eagerness feels like.
The TV blinks on the music channel,
switching from one generation of the gospel to another.
I call on the fertile seeds of motherhood
to pull the corners of my mouth high,
walk to my kids' room to see their little eyes
swagger open with mirth and glee.
I love how they show off for Mommy.

If I can just get to the house.
Makeup,
hair.
My arms are tired of lifting my fake confidence.
My face is tired of stretching to accommodate the lie.
I dress my outer shell in its most neutral attire—

nothing fancy, nothing plain,
just simple enough to give the impression I'm okay.

If I can just get to the house,
then I can breathe.
I can sit in the spot of prayer warriors before me
and let the echoes of their voices
speak the words my tongue chokes on.
I can bask in the overflow of glory and
let the oils fill my spirit until my hands
lift up in their own volition in praise.

If I can just get to the house,
I can get my breakthrough.

I Need a Word

I need a word spoken so bad I can feel the letters form in my belly, the syllables congregate in my throat, and taste victory on my tongue before the man of God even says hello.

I need a lesson flung across the pews so hard it knocks my common sense loose and sends it whirling into the atmosphere of praise so when it comes back to me, it's covered in faith.

I need a sermon preached so loud my 96-year-old future self can hear it over the sound of my great-grandchildren praying over my bed before I take my last breath.

I need a teacher to teach so well my 15-year-old self-inflicted wounds have no option other than to scar over and be the fertile ground from which purpose grows from pain.

I need a preacher to preach so good that the sweat from his brow flows like the blood dripping from calvary and covers every pew until the congregation is baptized anew.

I need an altar call so long it disrupts nature and surpasses kingdoms that even the animals repent for the violence between them.

I need a shut-in to go so in that the prayers we pray are buried in the fabric of the pews and the carpet becomes so infused with murmurings that the souls of our feet get saved as we walk.

I need a shout so loud that the heavens rejoice and the angels come down to stare in envy because they wish they had the Holy Ghost that's in me.

I need prayer so earnest, so earnest, that it reaches God's throne like a sweet-smelling colonge and he smiles at the sound of my adoration and love.

I need a fast so powerful that even the thought of the prayers in my mind becomes enough faith that God needs to move on my behalf.

I need a testimony shared so much that in my darkest days my soul is lifted by the memory of grace and it becomes the light I hold onto for my praise.

Oh I need... I need...

a word.

We Need to Be Aligned

My heart asked, what's wrong?
My mind said, I don't think we can do this.

Remember, we've always been strong.
I'm not really up to it.

You've come this far along.
But this requires more of me.

We can do this together.
I don't believe in anything.

I won't do this without you.
What do you want me to do?

God is telling us to move.
I feel so confused.

We have to be aligned.
Please, just give me more time.

Focus on this: Whatsoever, things are true.
Okay, I'll try. Whatsoever, things are honest…

Keep going.
Whatsoever, things are just—

He's always merciful to us.
Whatsoever, things are pure.

Let your peace be restored.
Whatsoever, things are lovely.

He said He will always love thee.
Whatsoever, things be of good report.

Let your faith rest assured.
If there be any virtue, if there be any praise.

Acknowledge the Lord in all your ways.
And think on these things.

Watch the joy it brings.

I'm not sure where I'm going.
You don't need to be.

I'm not sure how it will happen.
He's provided everything.

But I will step out on faith.
That's all He commands.

I will be sensitive to His tugging...

I will be obedient to His plan.

96

God, I Can Feel You

I can breathe you in
like a strong northern wind
enraptured around my soul.
It starts from my head and works it way down to my toes
to where every step I take is in the footprint of your sole.
Grace and mercy that have so far reached
past generations before me.
I know I am unworthy
yet here I am.

God, I can hear you,
loud as the rolling sea.
Waves crash against my mind, reforming words into poetry,
washing away doubt like sand to the open seas,
swallowing my fears til I stand here with certainty.
I am certain of you.

I can see you move,
clearing paths of my transgressions and rejections,
making detours for all my misdirections
so all roads lead back to life lessons
made into tangible expressions
of your love's perfection.

I can see you directing
me when to stop,
my knees to bend,

my hands to go up,
my mouth to breathe in.
my tongue to speak,
my head to bow,
my heart to open,
my feet to shout.

I can taste the victory in my mouth,
my praise dances on my tongue
as blood rushes to my fingertips,
showing stains of the battles overcome.
I can smell the bleeding heart of the son,
the flowing river of love's virtue
has encompassed me since day one.
God, I can sense you.

Sleep Comes

My nightmares faded
when I stopped being
scared of the pain.
Instead of running away,
I began to turn in.
Fists up,
feet wide and planted,
expecting the punch,
accepting the hurt
steeling the nerve
I bob and swerve
Making up my mind that,
win or survive
I will have the ~~fight~~
faith of my life.

Dear Girl,

Do it.
Gather to a place in yourself
where the quiet is fuel for your dreams.
Step out on faith
so that your purpose does not shame you.
Trust God to trust you with the lessons He taught you.
Stride into the meaning of your name.
This is not a season
but a continuation of the seed planted in you since birth.
A seed that has been choked on
by your refusal to unearth your hope.
There is more to your story.
Let your brief moment on Earth
be whispered forever in Heaven.
I love you for being broken
but not shattered.
This is not the year you make it.
Your hopes and dreams don't rest in a time frame—
a year is just a social construct.
But you,
dear girl,
are a whole entity
of power, light, and love.

Let Them

I say this with all the humility and love in my heart—move.
I am no longer apologizing for my body's womanly prowess.

Let the sun caress these curves
that bend like the initials of star, seed, and soul.
Let the moon rise over my dark skin's
smooth richness and luminous glow.
Let the wind flirt with my back
and cause goosebumps up and down my spine.
Let the river bend and twist
to mimic my tresses that grow as if designed.
Let the grass wave in appreciation
as they consider the sway of my hips.
Let the trees shake and shiver
from the tender graze of my skilled fingertips.
Let the bees buzz around my God-given bosom
that produces liquid gold.

Even fully clothed, I exude the femininity of divinity, and I
won't apologize for the masterpiece that is my womanhood.

Cat-calling in the Mirror

Hey, GIRL, hey!
I am doin it... I am it
the manifestation of my imagination
a love revelation from concerted effort and concentration
every tear I shed is dedicated to this moment
stand before my reflection and consciously own it
I've worked hard to get here
my process wasn't always clear but
it was divine
handcrafted
seconds of memories stitched together to shape the fabric of me
and boy am I expensive
I put time into this
I put life into this
I put fight into this
and I love all of it

I love the past me who didn't know better
I thought my father's actions echoed my worth
and I became perfect to prove I deserved space on earth
My tongue was once accustomed
to the salty taste of swallowing my words
and ballerinas used to envy how I tiptoed,
leaving eggshells undisturbed
I look back and marvel at how
I was able to hold such discontent
I guess, I confused it for humbleness

But yes, I still love that me
the unaware me
the scared me
the I would never dare me
the old me
alone me
the hideaway so no one would know me
the fat me
the black me
the one with crooked teeth and acne
the sad me
the glad me
the little girl staring right back at me
I love it all

I even love the now me
the proud me
still trying to figure it out me
the tall me
the strong me
you were beautiful all along me
the wife me
the mom me
the it's okay to be wrong me
the still me
the healed me
the vessel for God to fill me
I love it all

Who would have thought
I would get to the place of such acceptance
where I would gaze upon my scars
and not regret a single lesson
I would lust after my own body and revel in my own affection
That I would run my hands over the silhouette that is me,

Girl
Woman
Friend
Sister

And I would go through all those lessons again,
just to experience me

I Give You Permission

Let the walls explode
>and fall like confetti, making a pathway to the gates of
>heavenly acceptance.

Scream the words
>that make your heart stutter at the thought of them
>spraying from your lips like fragrances.

Fill the air
>with your confessions and make your heart lighter.

Spreadeagled
>in your puddle of tears and let it water your soul as
>you find strength in your surrender.

Tear it down,
>the destructive, carefully constructed behavior that
>has kept you imprisoned in the cycle of insanity.

Let it go,
>the notion that you are unloved and watch it float
>down to the hell from which it came.

Give it up,
>the idea that you are not enough, and watch it
>evaporate into thin air because there was never any
>truth in it anyway.

Let Him in.

He's been waiting for you to give him room to grow in your heart, to settle in your soul so he may find a home with you. Fill in the cracks of your spirit that left you feeling unwhole so he may be the source of your comfort. The prince of your peace.

I give you permission to try Him and see.

The Father Forgives

Dear God,

I come before you again,
as there has been this question burning in my mind.
I've been thinking this for a while,
and it may seem juvenile, but I'm curious:
What was the hardest part about the day
they hung you on the cross?

Not to diminish the suffering you experienced all along.
My thoughts are just on what must have been
the immeasurable burden of carrying the weight of such loss.

I couldn't imagine how it would feel
having to hear the callous words
of those who denied your deity,
or catch a glimpse of the man who betrayed you
out the side of your eye,
while fists and whips danced upon your back,
seducing life from your veins, your body used
as a receptacle for everyone else's pain
until you were unrecognizable.

Listen, I know you're God,

but in your humanity, I wonder which one was worse?
All the pain inflicted on your body
or all the ways your soul was hurt?

Not just from the deeds of those present but from the seeds of evil still left to sprout like weeds, growing in the garden of life, choking the beauty of it out, turning fields of newness into meadows of doubt. The ground still looks dry and barren because we walk as if the blood never poured out, trampling your name.

It's amazing to me,

how the abuse exercised upon your flesh was fleeting compared to the hundreds of years of continued theft of your holiness

The cat of nine tails can't compare
to the nine scales of narcissism we continue to embody.
We pluck out and criticize every fiber with passionate
fingertips, but call to you when we need somebody.
We spit upon your grace but demand
that you show us unmerited favor and mercy.
You laid naked and bare, patient and kind,
and many of us still deem you unworthy.
And all these years after crucifixion,
we still question if you are deserving of praise.
My God,
how did you not anger and rage
at those of us far off who were never in your presence,
but continued to whip you with the flick of our disgraceful
tongues dancing upon the essence of uncertainty,
arguing that your miracles may be more myth than reality?

And with all of that,
hanging on the horizon of your crucifixion,
I'm astounded that you say,
"Father, forgive them, for they know not what they do."
I can't imagine the pangs your heart must have been through.
Feeble minds can't comprehend the grace
that, in the moment of your weakness,
your face still bleeding,
your body still enduring,
your flesh still dying,
you thought enough of us to pray for our absolution
and, in your humiliation, provided restitution.

I wonder if having to let it go
was the toughest part of taking it on,
carrying the sins of an ungrateful creation
in your young, weakened arms.
See, the flesh can scar,
but a broken spirit is a death
in ways that change who you are.
That's what makes forgiveness so hard—
burying your ego so your soul can have a new start.

That must have been like a nail through the heart
of your humanity,
with no therapy,
no time to pass,
no process for grieving.
But you forgave us our future and our past.

I can only imagine that, on that day,
as you hung from your grave between dueling dimensions,
while Heaven applauded your sacrifice
and Earth debated your intentions,
it was the first time we witnessed a true resurrection of spirit,
where love ascended like doves,
cast dust to touch every one of us.
And it was on that day
you gave us hope that, while on this earth, we can begin anew.
After all our hurt, and pain, and shame,
our spirits can die only to be brought back to life.

Once we let it go
and untethered our souls from the grave of unforgiveness,
we can stop acting as if any one of us is sinless.

Gratitude

Thank you for your service.
Thank you for taking this young mind
and filling it with purpose.
Thank you for loving me despite
the times I've felt worthless.
Thank you for comforting me
when I didn't deserve it.
Thank you for the gift of life—
I've learned to preserve it.
Thank you for the process of pain—
it's been more than worth it

Thank you for sharing your humanity.
You've brought me so much clarity.
Thank you for having the patience,
pushing me past complacency.
Thank you for keeping me
when I didn't want to be kept.
Thank you for visiting my dreams,
for holding me while I slept.
Thank you for bringing peace
when I didn't understand.
Thank you for your friendship
before I had friends.
Thank you for never rescinding the gift.
You've always been my biggest blessing,
forever at my fingertips
Thank you.

ACKNOWLEDGMENTS

I want to start by thanking my husband, Kim, for holding down the fort when I cried, wrote, and zoned out while getting this book done. You are the real MVP, and I couldn't have done it without you. Thank you for always loving me and supporting me, no matter how crazy I can get. I love you to the moon and back.

I want to thank my kids, Micah and Aniyah, who are literally my favorite people in the world! Thank you for all the hugs and kisses and words of encouragement. You let Mommy write (half the time), and you always gave the best cuddles right before bed. I love you both.

I want to thank my mommy, Valencia. You have been such an integral part of my life and book. You are the one I confide in, cry too, talk with, laugh with. I honestly think we have one of the best mother-daughter relationships out there. You've supported me in my writing ever since I was a little girl, and I can't thank God enough for giving you to me as my mother.

I want to thank my step-dad, Cliff, for spoiling me and always treating me like I'm special. You are the best papa in the world!

I want to thank my dad, Derek, one of the most talented people I know, for giving me the gift of writing. You are a writer and have always been an inspiration to me. Thank you for loving me and rooting for me, even when I didn't root for myself.

I want to thank my brothers, Derek (DJ) and Jeremiah (Nunu), who have been by my side through it all. You make me laugh when I don't want to and you know how to put up with my extraness. Thank you for rooting me on during this process. And to all my siblings, Che, Rachel, Devin, David, Zion, Amara, Tanaya, Alex and CJ... I love you all. Thank you for being my family.

I want to thank my big cousin, LaShae, and my little cousin, Tori, who have been my loudest cheerleaders from the jump! You ladies hype me up, keep me grounded, and make me laugh. You've taught me the true meaning of sisterhood and friendship. Thank you.

I want to thank my aunties, Sheaton, Tracy, and Jan. I remember when I was little, the three of you would always tell me how good my writing was. I was always so talented in your eyes, and that meant so much to me. Thank you for being such great examples, leaders, and sources of encouragement to me.

I want to thank my grandmothers, Rachel (Grandma), Geraldine (Granny) and my grandfather (Graley) for all the unconditional love, soul food, and support. I love you both so much I can't even begin to describe it.

I want to thank my friends and coworkers, those near and

far, who always reminded me how important I am. You have made me feel loved and special even at my lowest times. I can't thank you enough.

I want to thank my church families for the values you have taught me. Thank you for the fellowship, the prayers, the Sunday School lessons, and the teachings.

I want to thank everyone at Community Literature Initiative. You have been the most interesting, supportive, thoughtful, and talented community I have ever been part of. Thank you to my classmates for sharing your journey with me. Thank you to my teachers, Andy Sanchez and Alex Petunia for being patient with me and giving me the best advice.

I want to thank the two biggest mentors I've had outside of my family, Sis Dean and Dr. B. You have both taught me so much about being a woman, a wife, and a child of God. I hold all your words of wisdom dear to my heart. Thank you for pouring them into me as a child and an adult. I love you both.

I want to thank Camari and Mama's Kitchen Press for believing in me. Our connection and work together has been so special to me. Thank you for holding space for my words and creating a platform for black poets everywhere. Your work is amazing and I am proud to say I am part of the Kitchen Krew!

Thank you to the reader for reading this book. Thank you for holding space for my words. I pray that God has been able to speak to you through this book. Let these poems come alive in your minds and help you in some way, draw you closer to Him.

Thank you all, and thank you, Jesus. Amen.

ABOUT THE POET

Tekira Briscoe is a millennial poet, writer, and creative with a passion for writing and storytelling. She hosts writing workshops and continues to perform on various stages around Los Angeles and elsewhere. She loves using her gift as a ministry to relate to and reach God's people. Sown in Light, her debut poetry collection, is a love letter to her youth, faith, and experience growing up in the Apostolic faith.

She currently resides in Los Angeles, California, with her loving and goofy husband, Kim, two kids, Micah and Aniyah, and two guinea pigs, Alex and Zachary.